# The Show-Biz Trivia Book

## by Mel Simons

Also by Mel Simons:

*The Old-Time Radio Trivia Book*

*The Old-Time Television Trivia Book*

*Old-Time Radio Memories*

# The Show-Biz Trivia Book

### by Mel Simons

BearManor Media
2007

The Show-Biz Trivia Book
Copyright © 2007 by Mel Simons


Printed in the United States of America

BearManor Media
P. O. Box 71426
Albany, GA  31708

bearmanormedia.com


Cover design by John Teehan

Typesetting and layout by John Teehan


ISBN—1-59393-134-4

# Dedication

*This book is dedicated to my uncle, Joe Bucks,*
*who sent me an accordion when I was 14 years old.*
*My life has not been the same since!*

*Mel Simons*

# Acknowledgements

My thanks to the Catholic Daughters of Brighton, Massachusetts. They hire me to entertain each year.

They recently made me an honorary member, which amazes me, since I am both male and Jewish!

# Foreword

As a fledgling radio announcer in Boston way back in the forties, one of my first assignments was a quiz show called *Depot Dialogues*, broadcast from the concourse of North Station.

Part of the job was to dream up a hundred and fifty simple questions a week.

"What was the color of Scarlett O'Hara's hair?" "What was the name of the Lone Ranger's horse?" That sort of thing.

Composing these "brain teasers" became an exhaustive chore for me, and I would have pounced on any of Mel Simons' books for help if they'd been around.

As you'll see in *The Show-Biz Trivia Book*, he's a master at digging up megastar minutiae on most any great performer, while jogging your memory at the same time. It's an art that puts him in a class by himself.

He's an enthusiastic interviewer, as I recently discovered as a guest on his radio show. His questions are brief but intelligent and provocative. His obvious interest leads the guest into a more intimate reflection of the guest's personality.

The tidbits inside are guaranteed to provide for fascinating fun, and a nostalgic trip, Mel Simons' trademark.

And—he can play the accordion...

—but only when requested to do so.

That, too, is class.

Bob Elliott
Bob and Ray

*Maurice Chevalier*

# Quiz #1

## MAURICE CHEVALIER
*(Answers on page 115)*

1. Name the city and country where Chevalier was born.
2. What was his age when he broke into show business?
3. What did he do?
4. What did he wear on his head?
5. What was his first hit record?
6. What was his biggest selling record?
7. Chevalier briefly appeared in what Marx Brothers movie?
8. Who was his co-star in the movie One Hour with You?
9. Name his best-selling autobiography.
10. *What song did Chevalier sing with Hermione Gingold in the movie Gigi?*

# Quiz #2

## Match the performer with his real name
*(Answers on page 115)*

1. Tony Curtis
2. Jack Palance
3. Frankie Valli
4. Mel Brooks
5. Alan King
6. Robert Alda
7. Harry Houdini
8. Engelbert Humperdinck
9. Boris Karloff
10. W.C. Fields

a. Erich Weiss
b. William Claude Dukenfield
c. Arnold Dorsey
d. Bernie Schwartz
e. Francis Stephen Castelluccio
f. Melvin Kaminsky
g. William Pratt
h. Irwin Kniberg
i. Alphonso D'Abruzzo
j. Volodymyr Palanyuk

# Quiz #3

## Match the television actor with his character

*(Answers on page 116)*

1. Robert Stack
2. Ted Knight
3. Jack Klugman
4. Ed Asner
5. Marvin Miller
6. Ralph Bellamy
7. Bob Crane
8. David Janssen
9. Wally Cox
10. Phil Silvers

a. Lou Grant
b. Sgt. Bilko
c. Mr. Peepers
d. Eliot Ness
e. Ted Baxter
f. Michael Anthony
g. Dr. Quincy
h. Dr. Richard Kimble
i. Col. Robert Hogan
j. Mike Barnett

*Jimmy Stewart*

# Quiz #4

## JIMMY STEWART
*(Answers on page 116)*

1. In what state was Jimmy born?

2. In 1935, Jimmy signed with what movie studio?

3. Jimmy won the Academy Award for what movie?

4. Jimmy became a Brigadier General in what branch of the service?

5. *Name the character he played in the movie,* It's a Wonderful Life.

6. Jimmy played what well-known orchestra leader in the movie of his life?

7. Jimmy played a clown in what movie?

8. How many times was Jimmy nominated for the Academy Award?

9. Jimmy starred in what radio show?

10. Doris Day co-starred with Jimmy in what Alfred Hitchcock movie?

# Quiz #5

## MUSICAL QUESTIONS
*(Answers on page 116)*

1. What singer and vocal group had a hit record with the song "Tammy"?

2. Name the accordionist who is identified with the song "Lady of Spain."

3. Who was the duo that had the number one record, "Vaya Con Dios"?

4. What singer was known as Miss Nibbs?

5. Who sang the vocal on Benny Goodman's recording of "And the Angels Sing"?

6. What sister vocal duo had the hit record "No More"?

7. Who was the first person elected to the Rock 'n' Roll Hall of Fame?

8. Who was known as the King of the Blues?

9. Name the Godfather of Soul.

10. *Who was the first act on* American Bandstand?

# Quiz #6

## COMEDY TEAMS
## Match the comic with his partner
*(Answers on page 117)*

1. Stan Laurel
2. Bud Abbott
3. Dean Martin
4. Fibber McGee
5. Phil Harris
6. Ole Olsen
7. Dan Rowan
8. George Burns
9. Joe Smith
10. Goodman Ace

a. Dick Martin
b. Gracie Allen
c. Lou Costello
d. Alice Faye
e. Oliver Hardy
f. Charlie Dale
g. Jerry Lewis
h. Molly
i. Chic Johnson
j. Jane

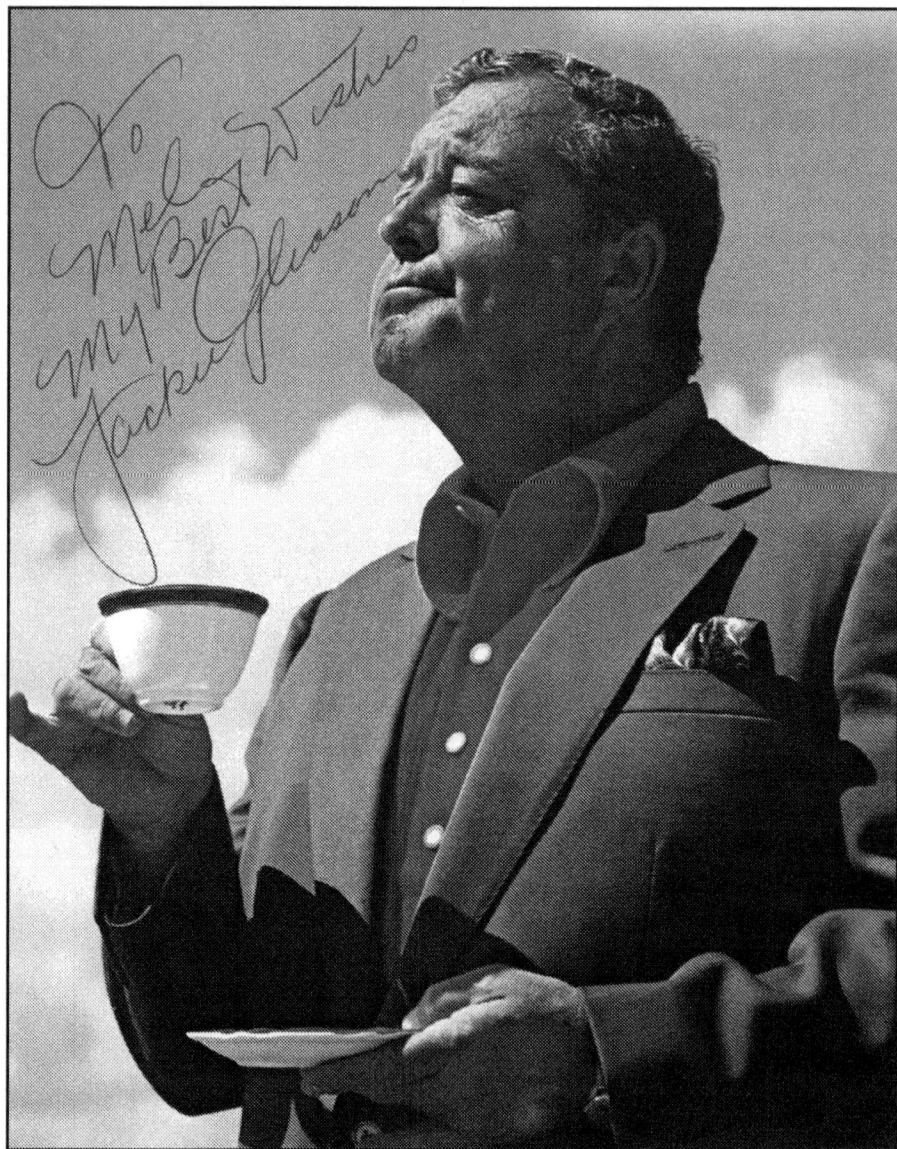

*Jackie Gleason*

# Quiz #7

## JACKIE GLEASON
*(Answers on page 117)*

1. What is Jackie's given name?

2. What did Jackie do before movies and television?

3. Jackie was in two movies with bandleader, Glenn Miller. Name them.

4. What was Jackie's first television show?

5. What was Jackie's first variety television show?

6. *Name the character that Art Carney played on* The Honeymooners.

7. Name the character that Frank Fontaine played.

8. Jackie played Minnesota Fats in what movie?

9. Who was the last Trixie?

10. What was Jackie's most famous catchphrase?

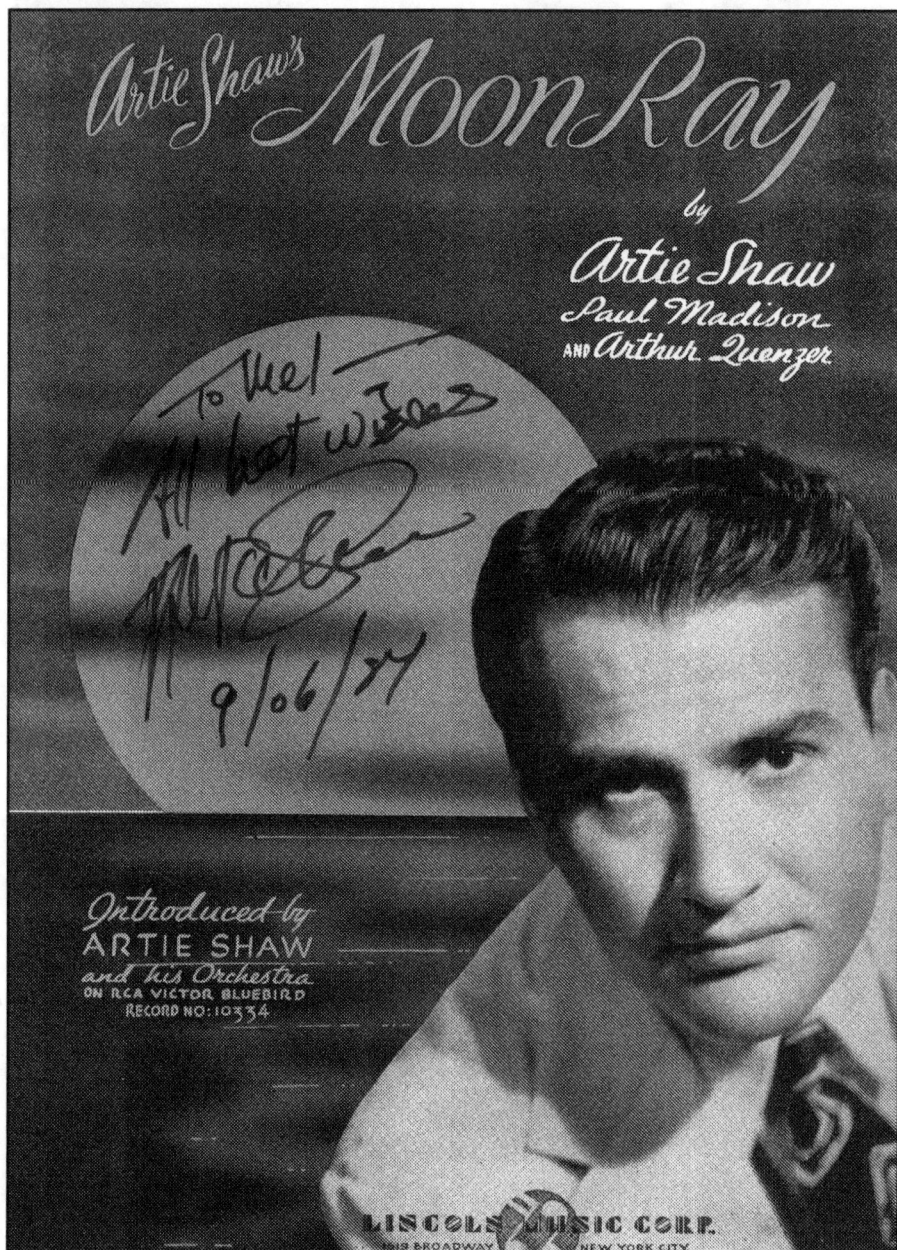

*Artie Shaw*

# Quiz #8

## What instrument did each bandleader play?
*(Answers on page 118)*

1. Ray Anthony
2. Tex Beneke
3. Eddie Duchin
4. Spike Jones
5. Buddy Morrow
6. Stan Kenton
7. Louie Prima
8. Wayne King
9. Ray McKinley
10. Clyde McCoy

# Quiz #9

**Match the Emmy Award-winning TV comedy show with the star**

*(Answers on page 118)*

1. Make Room for Daddy
2. Get Smart
3. All in the Family
4. M*A*S*H
5. Taxi
6. Barney Miller
7. Cheers
8. The Golden Girls
9. Murphy Brown
10. Frasier


a. Alan Alda
b. Don Adams
c. Ted Danson
d. Candice Bergen
e. Kelsey Grammer
f. Danny Thomas
g. Hal Linden
h. Bea Arthur
i. Carroll O'Conner
j. Judd Hirsch

# Quiz #10

## CARTOON QUESTIONS
*(Answers on page 118)*

1. Who was the voice of Bugs Bunny?
2. Little Lulu's best friend was…?
3. Name Popeye's girlfriend.
4. What cartoon character danced in the movie *Anchors Aweigh*?
5. Who was Mortimer Mouse?
6. What did Wimpy love to eat?
7. Jim Backus was the voice of who?
8. What was the first Mickey Mouse short?
9. Who was Sylvester always chasing?
10. Who provided the first voice for Elmer Fudd?

*John Wayne*

# Quiz #11

## JOHN WAYNE

*(Answers on page 119)*

1. What was John Wayne's real name?
2. Where did he grow up?
3. What was his famous nickname?
4. In high school, what sport did John excel in?
5. What college did he attend?
6. What cowboy got John his start in the movies?
7. Name the movie that made John a star.
8. Maureen O'Hara co-starred with John in what movies?
9. John won the Academy Award as Best Actor in what movie?
10. John had his biggest success with what motion picture company?

# Quiz #12

## Match the song with the movie
*(Answers on page 119)*

1. "More"
2. "Moon River"
3. "Can You Feel the Love Tonight?"
4. "Cheek to Cheek"
5. "Meet Me in St. Louis"
6. "I Can't Begin to Tell You"
7. "Bibbidi Bobbidi Boo"
8. "Hold My Hand"
9. "Something's Gotta Give"
10. "A Very Precious Love"

*a.* Breakfast at Tiffany's
*b.* Cinderella
*c.* Meet Me in St. Louis
*d.* The Dolly Sisters
*e.* Marjorie Morningstar
*f.* Daddy Long Legs
*g.* Mondo Cane
*h.* Top Hat
*i.* The Lion King
*j.* Susan Slept Here

# Quiz #13

## Match the Grammy Award Record of the Year with the artist

*(Answers on page 120)*

1. "Mack the Knife"
2. "Strangers in the Night"
3. "Mrs. Robinson"
4. "I Left My Heart in San Francisco"
5. "The First Time Ever I Saw Your Face"
6. "Volare"
7. "Love Will Keep Us Together"
8. "Up, Up and Away"
9. "A Taste of Honey"
10. "Theme from A Summer Place"

a. Tony Bennett
b. Simon and Garfunkle
c. Frank Sinatra
d. The Captain and Tennille
e. The Fifth Dimension
f. Roberta Flack
g. Domenico Modugno
h. Herb Alpert
i. Bobby Darin
j. Percy Faith

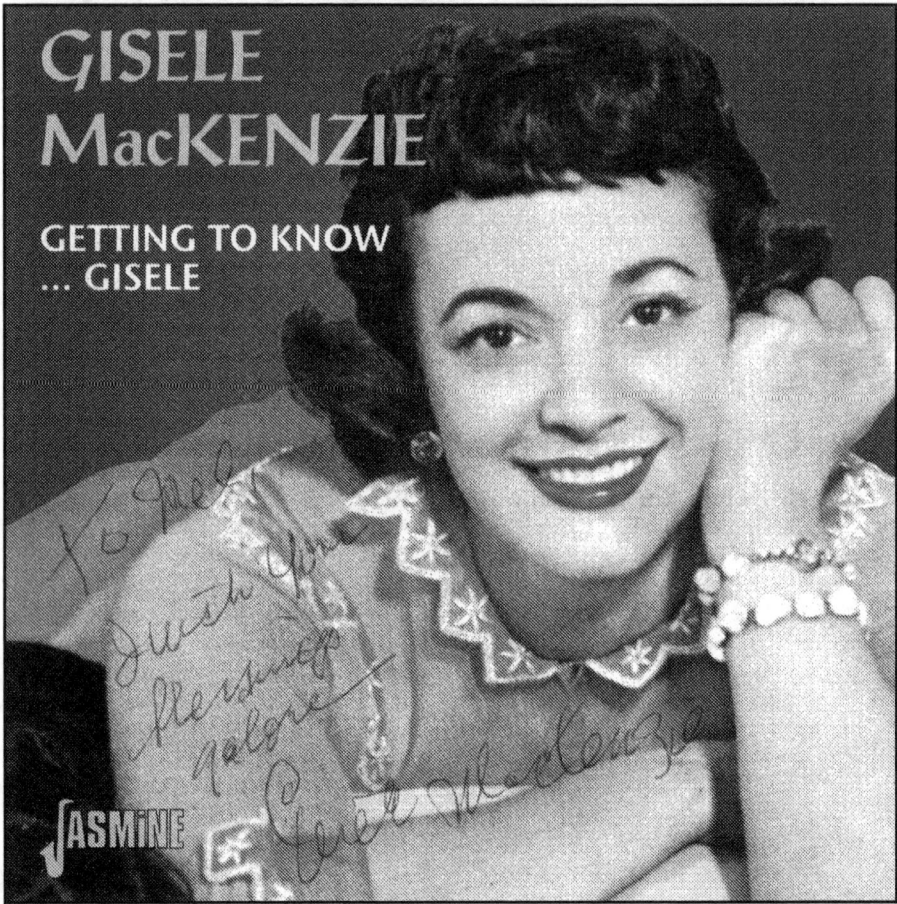

*Gisele MacKenzie*

# Quiz #14

## ONE HIT WONDERS
## Match the singers with their only hit record
*(Answers on page 120)*

1.  "Those Were the Days"
2.  "You Light Up My Life"
3.  "Band of Gold"
4.  "Let Me Go Lover
5.  "Eve of Destruction"
6.  "I'm Gonna Sit Right Down and Write Myself a Letter"
7.  "Ringo"
8.  "Hard to Get"
9.  "Abraham, Martin, and John"
10. "The Night the Lights Went Out in Georgia"

a.  Moms Mabley
b.  Lorne Greene
c.  Barry McGuire
d.  Don Cherry
e.  Debby Boone
f.  Vicki Lawrence
g.  Mary Hopkins
h.  Joan Weber
i.  Gisele MacKenzie
j.  Billy Williams

*Debby Boone*

# Quiz #15

## FAMOUS NIGHTCLUBS
## Name the city where each nightclub was located.
*(Answers on page 120)*

1. Copacabana
2. Blinstrubs
3. Palmer House
4. Latin Casino
5. Holiday House
6. Town Casino
7. Desert Inn
8. Town and Country Club
9. Mr. Kelly's
10. Elmwood Casino

*Frank Sinatra*

# Quiz #16

## FRANK SINATRA

*(Answers on page 121)*

1. What was Frank's middle name?

2. What was the name of Frank's original vocal group?

3. In 1935 Frank appeared on a famous radio show. Name the show.

4. How many times was Frank married?

5. Frank had how many children?

6. Name the two big bands that Frank sang with.

7. As a big band singer, what was Frank's biggest hit record?

8. Name the popular radio show that Frank sang on in the 1940s.

9. *Frank won the Academy Award as Best Supporting Actor in the movie* From Here to Eternity. *Name the character that he played.*

10. What was Frank's last number one record?

*The Platters*

# Quiz #17

**Match the rock 'n' roll group with the lead singer**
*(Answers on page 121)*

1. Frankie Valli
2. Paul Revere
3. Harold Melvin
4. Patty LaBelle
5. Jay Black
6. Freddie
7. Duanne Eddy
8. Herman
9. Kenny Rogers
10. Tony Williams


a. First Edition
b. The Americans
c. The Four Seasons
d. The Blue Belles
e. The Blue Notes
f. The Hermits
g. The Platters
h. The Rebels
i. The Dreamers
j. The Raiders

*Killer Kowalski*

# Quiz #18

## PRO WRESTLING
## (It's really Show-Biz!!)
*(Answers on page 122)*

1. What wrestler was known as "The Animal"?

2. Who won most of his matches using "The Claw Hold"?

3. Name the two wrestlers who used the phrase "Nature Boy."

4. Where was Antonino Rocca from?

5. Who was Joe Scarpa?

6. Who was George Wagner?

7. Name the 7-ft.-4-inch giant from France.

8. Who was the longest-running WWF Champion?

9. Who was the longest-running NWA Champion?

10. Bruno Sammartino won most of his matches using what hold?

*Bing Crosby*

# Quiz #19

## BING CROSBY
*(Answers on page 122)*

1. Where was Bing born?
2. What is his real name?
3. Bing's first claim to fame was singing with what famous band?
4. With that band, he sang with Al Rinker and Harry Barris. What were they called?
5. Name Bing's two wives.
6. How many children did Bing have?
7. Bing won the Academy Award as Best Actor in what movie?
8. What type of role did he play in the movie?
9. In the 1960s, Bing often hosted what television show?
10. What was the biggest hit record that Bing had?

# Quiz #20

## Match the television actress with her character
*(Answers on page 122)*

1.  Eve Arden
2.  Vivian Vance
3.  Amanda Blake
4.  Barbara Feldon
5.  Barbara Britton
6.  Marie Wilson
7.  Nancy Walker
8.  Angie Dickinson
9.  Isabel Sanford
10. Betty Garrett

a.  Louise Jefferson
b.  Agent 99
c.  Pepper Anderson
d.  Ethel Mertz
e.  Connie Brooks
f.  Kitty Russell
g.  Irene Lorenzo
h.  Ida Morgenstern
i.  Pamela North
j.  Irma Peterson

# Quiz #21

## OLD-TIME RADIO QUESTIONS
*(Answers on page 123)*

1. Who was the All-American Boy?
2. What radio show became a comic strip and a Broadway show?
3. On *The Judy Canova Show* who played Pedro?
4. What vocal group sang the commercials on *The Jack Benny Program*?
5. Who replaced Frank Sinatra on *Your Hit Parade*?
6. What was the name of the doctor on *Fibber McGee & Molly*?
7. Name the female vocal group on *The Fred Allen Show*.
8. What musical instrument did Rosa Rio play?
9. Who was Mike Waring?
10. On *A Date with Judy*, who was Judy's boyfriend?

*Edgar Bergen*

*Paul Winchell*

# Quiz #22

## Match the ventriloquist and the dummy

*(Answers on page 123)*

1. Edgar Bergen
2. Paul Winchell
3. Senor Wences
4. Ricky Lane
5. Shari Lewis
6. Willie Tyler
7. Wayland Flowers
8. Jimmy Nelson
9. Jeff Dunham
10. Ronn Lucas

a. Lamb Chop
b. Knucklehead Smiff
c. Effie Klinker
d. Lester
e. Velvel
f. Peanut
g. Pedro
h. Buffalo Billy
i. Farfel
j. Madame

*Edgar Bergen*

# Quiz #23

## Match the Tony Award-winning actor with the Broadway musical

*(Answers on page 124)*

1. Gregory Hines
2. Jim Dale
3. Robert Goulet
4. Zero Mostel
5. Jane Alexander
6. Ben Vereen
7. Hal Linden
8. Phil Silvers
9. Jerry Orbach
10. Robert Preston

a. *Promises, Promises*
b. Fiddler on the Roof
c. *Pippin*
d. I Do! I Do!
e. *Jelly's Last Jam*
f. *The Rothchilds*
g. *Barnum*
h. *The Happy Time*
i. *Jerome Robbins' Broadway*
j. *A Funny Thing Happened on the Way to the Forum*

*Charlie Chaplin*

# Quiz #24

## CHARLIE CHAPLIN
*(Answers on page 124)*

1.  What was Chaplin's character known as?
2.  Who hired Chaplin for the movies?
3.  What was his first one-reel movie?
4.  In 1919 Chaplin started United Artists with what three film giants?
5.  In what movie did Charlie eat his shoes and shoelaces?
6.  What was Chaplin's last silent movie?
7.  Chaplin played a Hitler-like character in what movie?
8.  What movie did Chaplin make with Buster Keaton as his co-star?
9.  Chaplin wrote many songs. What was his biggest hit?
10. Who played Chaplin in the movie of his life?

*Neil Sedaka*

# Quiz #25

## NAME THE NEIL
## Is it Neil Diamond or Neil Sedaka?
*(Answers on page 124)*

1. Who came from Brooklyn?
2. Who attended Abraham Lincoln High School?
3. Who had a scholarship to Julliard School of Music?
4. Who wrote the song "Stupid Cupid" for Connie Francis?
5. Who wrote the song "Laughter in the Rain"?
6. Who wrote the song "I'm a Believer" for the Monkees?
7. Who wrote the song "Love on the Rocks"?
8. In 1962, who married his wife, Leba?
9. Who wrote the song "Love Will Keep Us Together" for The Captain and Tennille?
10. Who had the most #1 records?

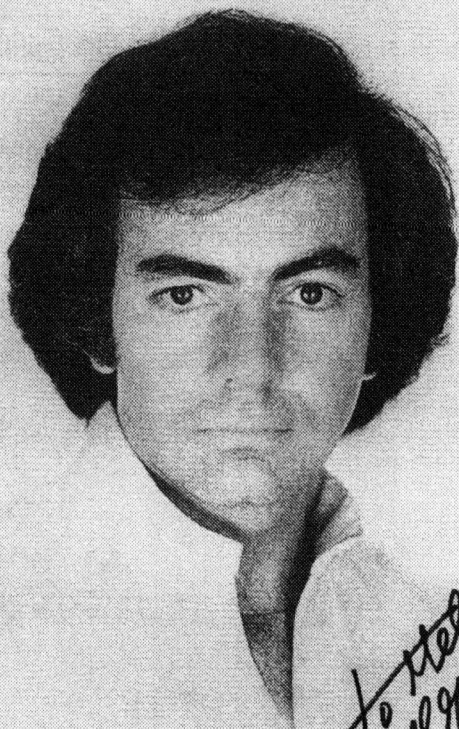

*Neil Diamond*

# Quiz #26

## JAY LENO & DAVID LETTERMAN
## Is it Jay or David?
*(Answers on page 125)*

1. Who has a gap between his two front teeth?
2. Who was born in Andover, Mass.?
3. Who has hosted a television show the longest?
4. Whose mother wrote a cookbook?
5. Who filled in the most for Johnny Carson?
6. Who once hosted the Academy Awards?
7. Who has the most children?
8. Who once hosted a daytime television show?
9. Who was in the movie *American Graffiti*?
10. Who once wrestled in a pro match?

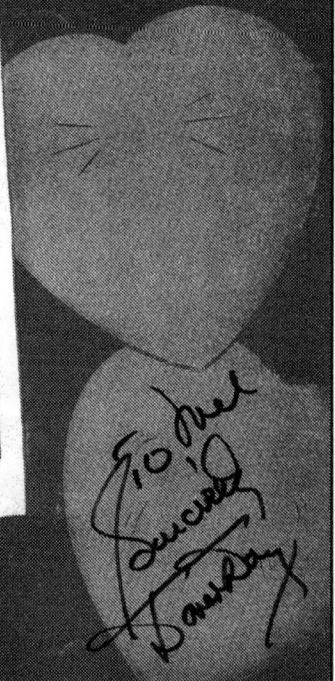

*Doris Day*

# Quiz #27

## DORIS DAY

*(Answers on page 126)*

1. What did Doris take up before she became a singer?
2. Name the three big bands that Doris sang with.
3. In 1945, Doris had two #1 records. Name them.
4. Name the Alfred Hitchcock movie that Doris starred in.
5. Frank Sinatra co-starred with Doris in what movie?
6. Name the Academy Award-winning song that Doris sang in the movie *Calamity Jane*.
7. Name the Academy Award-winning song that Doris sang in the movie *The Man Who Knew Too Much*.
8. On *The Doris Day Television Show*, what was her character's name?
9. In the movie *Love Me or Leave Me*, what old-time singer did she portray?
10. What was Doris' last top ten record?

*Ernest Borgnine*

# Quiz #28

## Match the Academy Award-winning actor with the movie

*(Answers on page 126)*

1. Rod Steiger
2. Fredric March
3. Peter Finch
4. Sidney Poitier
5. Ernest Borgnine
6. Paul Muni
7. William Holden
8. Cliff Robertson
9. Gary Cooper
10. Dustin Hoffman

a. *The Best Years of Our Lives*
b. *Network*
c. *Kramer vs. Kramer*
d. *In the Heat of the Night*
e. *Stalag 17*
f. *Charly*
g. *Sergeant York*
h. *Lillies of the Field*
i. *The Story of Louis Pasteur*
j. *Marty*

# Quiz #29

## OLD-TIME RADIO QUESTIONS
*(Answers on page 126)*

1.  Who played Baby Snooks on radio?
2.  What was the name of Jack Benny's car?
3.  Who sponsored *The Phil Harris/Alice Faye Show*?
4.  Who was Mr. Keen's assistant?
5.  Who was the first host of the *Lux Radio Theater*?
6.  Marie Wilson played what character on *My Friend Irma*?
7.  Who hosted the *Lemac Show*?
8.  Who was married to Goodman Ace?
9.  Steve Wilson was a character on what show?
10. The Fat Man was played by whom?

# Quiz #30

## VAUDEVILLE

*(Answers on page 127)*

1. Name the most famous vaudeville theater in the United States.

2. What was the most lavish show on Broadway?

3. Who was the last of the red hot mamas?

4. What did W.C. Fields do in vaudeville?

5. Who said, "Is everybody happy?"

6. Who was known as "Banjo Eyes"?

7. What vaudeville comedian was married to Barbara Stanwyck?

8. What was the name of the Marx Brothers' mother?

9. Who spun a lariat and read from a newspaper?

10. Who was the first comedian to use a telephone as a prop?

*Ginger Rogers and Fred Astaire*

# Quiz #31

## FRED ASTAIRE or GENE KELLY
## Was it Fred or Gene?
*(Answers on page 127)*

1. Who taught Frank Sinatra how to dance?
2. Who graduated from the University of Pittsburgh?
3. Who danced with a coat rack?
4. Who had a sister named Adele?
5. Who did many television specials?
6. Who appeared in the movie *On the Beach*?
7. Who narrated the movie *That's Entertainment*?
8. Who starred in the movie *Marjorie Morningstar*?
9. Who directed the movie *Hello, Dolly*?
10. Whose studio report on his first screen test read: "Can't act, can't sing, can dance a little"?

YOU WONDERFUL YOU
Lyric by JACK BROOKS and SAUL CHAPLIN
Music by HARRY WARREN
JUDY GARLAND
GENE KELLY
M-G-M's
SUMMER STOCK
CO-STARRING
EDDIE BRACKEN · GLORIA DE HAVEN · MARJORIE MAIN · PHIL SILVERS
RAY COLLINS
TECHNICOLOR
CHARLES WALTERS · JOE PASTERNAK
A METRO-GOLDWYN-MAYER PICTURE
MILLER MUSIC CORPORATION
799 SEVENTH AVENUE · NEW YORK 19, N. Y.
SONGS
YOU WONDERFUL YOU
DIG-DIG-DIG FOR YOUR DINNER

*Gene Kelly*

# Quiz #32

## Match the song with the Broadway show
*(Answers on page 128)*

1.  "Get Me to the Church on Time"
2.  "Sunrise, Sunset"
3.  "Getting to Know You"
4.  "The Best of Times"
5.  "Edelweiss"
6.  "Hey, Look Me Over"
7.  "Some Enchanted Evening"
8.  "Just in Time"
9.  "All of You"
10. "Almost Like Being in Love"

a.  *South Pacific*
b.  *The Sound of Music*
c.  *Silk Stockings*
d.  *Fiddler on the Roof*
e.  *My Fair Lady*
f.  *Wildcat*
g.  *The King and I*
h.  *Le Cage Aux Folles*
i.  *Bells Are Ringing*
j.  *Brigadoon*

*Mae West*

# Quiz #33

## Match the catchphrase with the comedienne
*(Answers on page 128)*

1. "Ohhh, Rob!"
2. "My husband, Fang…"
3. "I've been on a diet for two weeks, and all I lost was fourteen pounds!"
4. "Why don't you come up and see me some time?"
5. "Can we talk!"
6. "One ringee dingee…two ringee dingees."
7. "Yoo-hoo, is anybody?"
8. "An old man can't do nothin' for me, except to bring me a message from a young man."
9. "My brother, Willie."
10. "Hey, Daddy!"

*The Three Stooges*

# Quiz #34

## THE THREE STOOGES
*(Answers on page 128)*

1. Who created and was the original leader of the Stooges?
2. The three Howard brothers, Moe, Curly, and Shemp— what were their birth names?
3. What was Larry Fine's real name?
4. What musical instrument did Larry play?
5. How many shorts did the Stooges make for Columbia Pictures?
6. What year did Shemp leave the Stooges, and what year did he return?
7. Which Stooge said, "Nyuk, nyuk, nyuk!"?
8. Which Stooge said, "Not so hard...!"?
9. Who was the last comedian to join the Stooges, and what was his real name?
10. What the Stooges' first theme song?

*Cary Grant*

# Quiz #35

## CARY GRANT
*(Answers on page 129)*

1.  How many times was Cary nominated for the Academy Award?

2.  Name the four movies that he did for Alfred Hitchcock.

3.  In what Hitchcock movie did a plane chase him?

4.  Name the movie that Cary starred in with Doris Day.

5.  In 1970 Cary received an Honorary Academy Award for Lifetime Achievement. Who presented him with the award?

6.  Grace Kelly appeared with Cary in what movie?

7.  How many times was Cary married?

8.  Which one of his wives was a wealthy socialite?

9.  Cary's fourth wife was a well-known actress. Who was she?

10. How many children did Cary have?

# Quiz #36

## COWBOY QUESTIONS
*(Answers on page 129)*

1. Who was the Range Rider?
2. What was Hopalong Cassidy's real name?
3. Pat Buttram was a sidekick to whom?
4. What was the longest running Western on television?
5. What was the second longest running Western on television?
6. Who was the star of radio's *Melody Ranch*?
7. What cowboy used a whip?
8. Who was Hopalong Cassidy's sidekick?
9. Who played that character?
10. Name the family on *Bonanza*.

# Quiz #37

## Match the performer with her real name
*(Answers on page 130)*

1. Shelley Winters
2. Dagmar
3. Piper Laurie
4. Jane Wyman
5. Beverly Sills
6. Stefanie Powers
7. Sophie Tucker
8. June Allyson
9. Judy Holliday
10. Diane Keaton

a. Shirley Schrift
b. Ava Gardner
c. Virginia Ruth Egnor
d. Judith Tuvim
e. Diane Hall
f. Belle Silverman
g. Rosetta Jacobs
h. Ella Geisman
i. Stefania Zofya Federkiewicz
j. Sophie Kalish

*Jimmy Durante*

# Quiz #38

## JIMMY DURANTE
*(Answers on page 130)*

1. What was Jimmy's nickname?
2. Name his signature song.
3. In vaudeville, name Jimmy's trio.
4. Jimmy once owned a nightclub. What was it called?
5. Who was Jimmy's co-host on radio?
6. What Billy Rose Broadway show did Jimmy star in?
7. In 1962, Jimmy appeared in what movie with Doris Day?
8. What was Jimmy's last hit record?
9. What was the last movie that Jimmy appeared in?
10. Who did Jimmy always say goodnight to?

The Mills Brothers

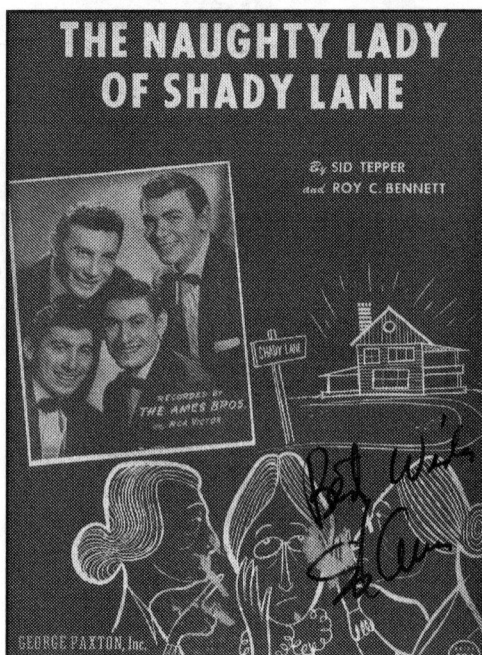

The Four Lads

The Ames Brothers

# Quiz #39

**THE FABULOUS FOURS**
**What four-man group had these hit records?**
*(Answers on page 130)*

1. "Stranger in Paradise"
2. "No, Not Much"
3. "You, You, You"
4. "Love Is a Many Splendored Thing"
5. "Big Man"
6. "Naughty Lady of Shady Lane"
7. "Standing on the Corner"
8. "Twenty-Six Miles"
9. "Shangri-La"
10. "Three Coins in a Fountain"

# Quiz #40

## COMEDIAN QUESTIONS
*(Answers on page 131)*

1. Eve Arden starred in what radio and television show?
2. What was her profession?
3. Who played The Mad Russian?
4. Danny Kaye was married to whom?
5. What comedian would always say, "Post time!"?
6. What comedian starred in TV's *I Spy*?
7. Who was Ish Kabbible?
8. Whose mouth was compared to the Grand Canyon?
9. What comedian was a Spanish Teacher?
10. On the television show *I Married Joan*, what was Joan's husband's name?

# Quiz #41

## Match the rock 'n' roll group with the lead singer
*(Answers on page 131)*

1. Bruce Springsteen
2. Danny
3. Country Joe
4. Wayne Cochran
5. Dion
6. Buddy Holly
7. Jr. Walker
8. Dr. Hook
9. John Mayall
10. Dennis Yost

a. The Classic IV
b. The Bluesbreakers
c. Medicine Show
d. All-Stars
e. The Crickets
f. The Belmonts
g. C. C. Riders
h. The Fish
i. The Juniors
j. The E Street Band

*Stan Laurel and Oliver Hardy*

# Quiz #42

## STAN LAUREL & OLIVER HARDY
*(Answers on page 132)*

1.  What year did Stan and Ollie become a team?
2.  Early in his career, Stan was an understudy to what famous comedian?
3.  What is Oliver Hardy's real first name?
4.  What was Hardy's nickname?
5.  Which of the two was a trained singer?
6.  Laurel and Hardy won the Academy Award for Best Short Subject. Name the movie and the year.
7.  Name Laurel and Hardy's theme song.
8.  Who created most of their comedy bits?
9.  Who was their most successful producer?
10. What is the name of the Laurel and Hardy fan club?

*Les Brown*

# Quiz #43

## Match the bandleader with his theme song

*(Answers on page 132)*

1. Lawrence Welk
2. Count Basie
3. Harry James
4. Ray Anthony
5. Duke Ellington
6. Les Brown
7. Les Elgart
8. Stan Kenton
9. Wayne King
10. Henry Busse

a. "Take the A Train"
b. "Bubbles in the Wine"
c. "Young Man with a Horn"
d. "Ciribiribin"
e. "Leap Frog"
f. "One O'Clock Jump"
g. "Hot Lips"
h. "The Waltz You Saved for Me"
i. "Artistry in Rhythm"
j. "Sophisticated Swing"

*Eddie Cantor*

# Quiz #44

**EDDIE CANTOR**

*(Answers on page 132)*

1. What was Eddie's real name?
2. He was married to who?
3. What was Eddie's nickname?
4. Who gave Eddie his big break?
5. What year did Eddie begin in the *Ziegfeld Follies*?
6. What was the first national radio show on which Eddie appeared?
7. On his radio show, Eddie founded what charitable organization?
8. Eddie discovered and introduced what famous female singer?
9. Eddie was a regular on what television show?
10. In the movie, *The Eddie Cantor Story*, who played Eddie?

# Quiz #45

## Match the song with the composer
*(Answers on page 133)*

1. "Put Your Head on My Shoulder"
2. "Breaking Up Is Hard To Do"
3. "Five Minutes More"
4. "Over the Rainbow"
5. "Lullabye of Broadway"
6. "Ain't Misbehavin'"
7. "I Could Write a Book"
8. "I Could Have Danced All Night"
9. "Over There"
10. "Alfie"

a. George M. Cohan
b. Fats Waller and Harry Brooks
c. Harold Arlen and E.Y Harburg
d. Al Dubin and Harry Warren
e. Lorenz Hart and Richard Rogers
f. Sammy Cahn and Jule Styne
g. Alan Jay Lerner and Frederick Loewe
h. Neil Sedaka and Howard Greenfield
i. Paul Anka
j. Hal David and Burt Bacharach

# Quiz #46

## Match the performer with her real name
*(Answers on page 133)*

1. Kaye Ballard
2. Vivian Blaine
3. Marilyn Monroe
4. Joan Rivers
5. Gloria Swanson
6. Abigail Van Buren
7. Natalie Wood
8. Ginger Rogers
9. Sophia Loren
10. Crystal Gayle

a. Joan Molinsky
b. Sofia Villani Scicolone
c. Natalia Nikolaevna Zakharenko
d. Gloria May Josephine Svensson
e. Virginia McMath
f. Brenda Gail Webb
g. Catherine Gloria Balotta
h. Pauline Esther Friedman
i. Vivian Stapleton
j. Norma Jean Baker

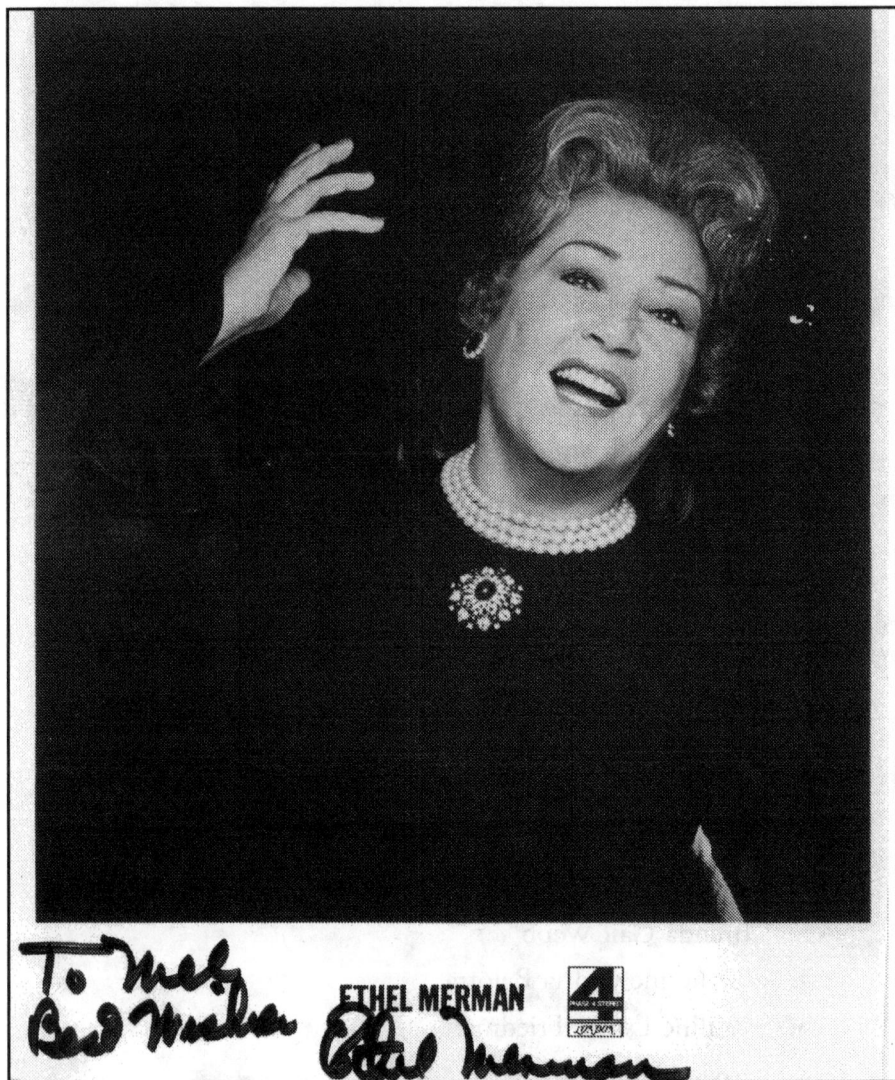

*Ethel Merman*

# Quiz #47

## ETHEL MERMAN & MARY MARTIN
## Was it Ethel or Mary?

*(Answers on page 134)*

1. Whose real last name was Zimmerman?
2. Who was born in Astoria, New York?
3. Who was born in Texas?
4. Who sang "My Heart Belongs to Daddy"?
5. Who was briefly married to Ernest Borgnine?
6. Who starred in *Peter Pan*?
7. Who starred in *South Pacific*?
8. Who got their big break in *Girl Crazy*?
9. Who appeared in the movie, *It's a Mad, Mad, Mad, Mad World*?
10. Whose trademark song is "There's No Business Like Show Business"?

*Mary Martin*

# Quiz #48

## OLD-TIME RADIO QUESTIONS
*(Answers on page 134)*

1.   On the radio show *Life with Luigi*, what did Luigi do for a living?
2.   What was the name of The Great Gildersleeve's maid?
3.   Who was Henry Aldrich's best friend?
4.   What was Johnny Dollar's profession?
5.   Who played Sgt. Joe Friday?
6.   What comedian played the bazooka?
7.   Who was the sponsor on *Arthur Godfrey's Talent Scouts*?
8.   What show did the Man in Black host?
9.   On *The Fred Allen Show*, who played Mrs. Nussbaum?
10.  Who called for Philip Morris?

*Don Rickles*

# Quiz #49

## Match the comedian with his catch phrase
*(Answers on page 134)*

1. "Hey, Abbottttttt!"
2. "I'll be a dirty bird."
3. "Yoo hoo, it's me."
4. "I kid you not!"
5. "I'm a wild and crazy guy!"
6. "Duffy ain't here."
7. "I got a letter from mama."
8. "So I ups to him."
9. "Up your nose with a rubber hose."
10. "You dummy."

a. Steve Martin
b. Don Rickles
c. Pinky Lee
d. Gabe Kaplan
e. Lou Costello
f. Jimmy Durante
g. Charlie Weaver
h. Ed Gardner
i. Jack Paar
j. George Gobel

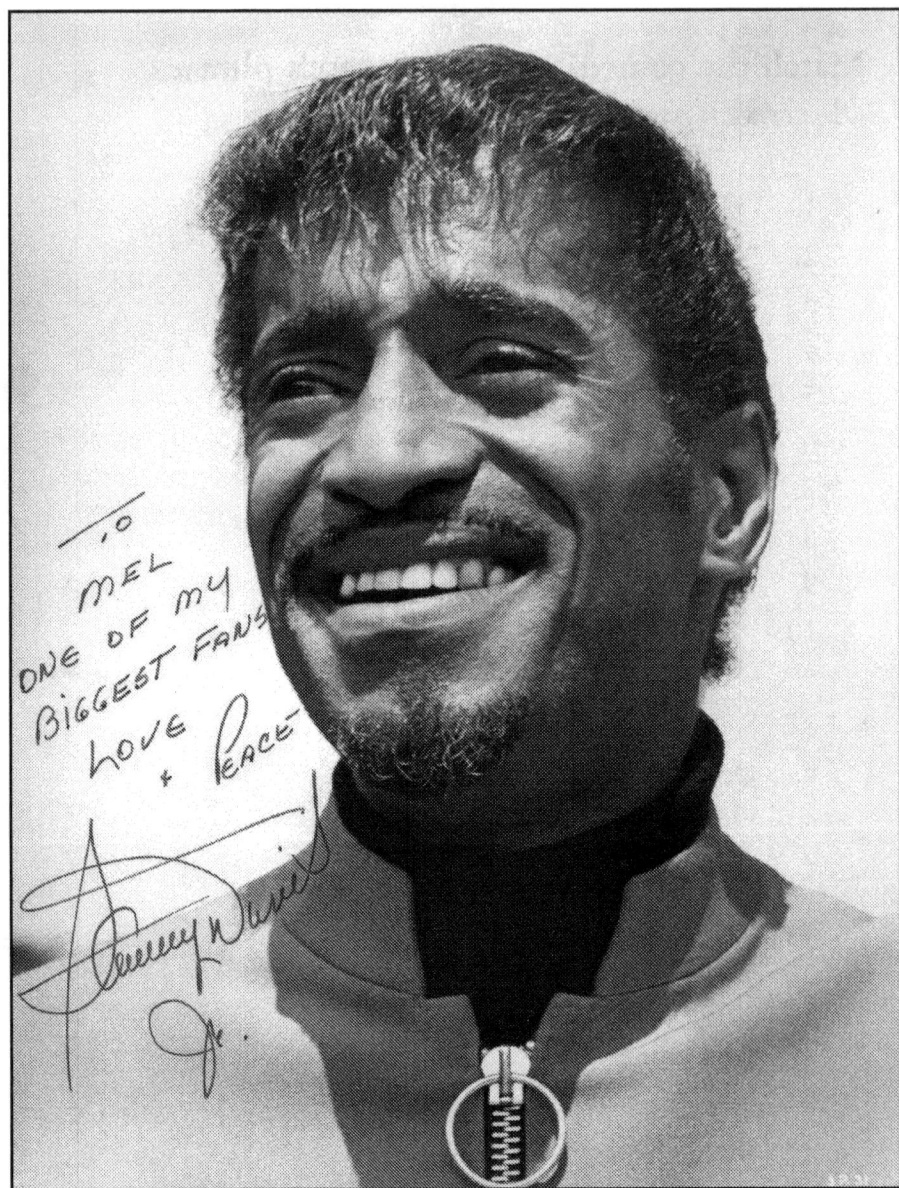

*Sammy Davis, Jr.*

# Quiz #50

## SAMMY DAVIS, JR.
*(Answers on page 135)*

1.  In what year was Sammy born?
2.  Who taught Sammy how to dance?
3.  Name the trio that Sammy began his career with.
4.  Name Sammy's first Broadway show.
5.  Name the group, led by Frank Sinatra, that Sammy became a member of.
6.  What religion did Sammy convert to?
7.  What was the title of Sammy's first autobiography?
8.  Name Sammy's two wives.
9.  Sammy received a Tony nomination for what Broadway show?
10. Sammy had one #1 record. What was it?

# Quiz #51

## Match the comedian with his catch phrase
*(Answers on page 135)*

1.  "My name Jose Jimenez."
2.  "Hey, Mr. Benny."
3.  "Never got a dinner."
4.  "Say goodnight, Gracie."
5.  "Here's another nice mess you've gotten me into."
6.  "Sorry about that, Chief."
7.  "Now cut that out!"
8.  "Mom always liked you better."
9.  "Glad to see ya."
10. "Post time!"


a.  Bill Dana
b.  George Burns
c.  Tom Smothers
d.  Rochester
e.  Red Buttons
f.  Oliver Hardy
g.  Phil Silvers
h.  Joe E. Lewis
i.  Jack Benny
j.  Don Adams

# Quiz #52

## Match the Academy Award-winning song with the movie

*(Answers on page 136)*

1. "Chim Chim Cher-ee"
2. "Buttons and Bows"
3. "Whatever Will Be, Will Be (Que Sera, Sera)"
4. "The Way You Look Tonight"
5. "Call Me Irresponsible"
6. "Do Not Forsake Me"
7. "Zip-A-Dee-Doo-Dah"
8. "The Last Time I Saw Paris"
9. "It Might As Well Be Spring"
10. "In the Cool, Cool, Cool of the Evening"

a. *The Man Who Knew Too Much*
b. *High Noon*
c. *Mary Poppins*
d. *State Fair*
e. *Here Comes the Groom*
f. *Paleface*
g. *Song of the South*
h. *Swing Time*
i. *Lady Be Good*
j. *Papa's Delicate Condition*

*James Cagney*

# Quiz #53

## JAMES CAGNEY
*(Answers on page 136)*

1.  Where was Cagney born?

2.  What did he do before making movies?

3.  How tall was Cagney?

4.  What was Cagney's first tough guy movie?

5.  What unusual thing did Cagney do to Mae Clarke in that movie?

6.  Name the movie for which Cagney won the Academy Award as Best Actor.

7.  What famous entertainer did he play in that movie?

8.  In what movie did Cagney say, "You dirty rat!"?

9.  Name Cagney's sister, who was an actress.

10. Cagney co-starred with Doris Day in what movie?

# Quiz #54

## SILENT MOVIES
*(Answers on page 136)*

1. Who played the Little Tramp?
2. Name the most popular comedy team.
3. Who was "the It Girl"?
4. Who was the Man of a Thousand Faces?
5. What was the first film ever made?
6. Who was America's Sweetheart?
7. What was the name of Lillian Gish's sister?
8. Who was the master of the slow burn?
9. Who starred in *The Perils of Pauline*?
10. What comedian never smiled?

# Quiz #55

## Match the performer with his real name
*(Answers on page 137)*

1. Cary Grant
2. Pinky Lee
3. Tony Martin
4. Jack Oakie
5. Tony Randall
6. Omar Sharif
7. Ringo Starr
8. Lenny Bruce
9. Orson Bean
10. Rex Harrison

a. Richard Starkey
b. Leonard Rosenberg
c. Dallas F. Burrows
d. Archibald Leach
e. Alfred Schneider
f. Reginald Carey
g. Pincus Leff
h. Alvin Morris
i. Michael Shalhoub
j. Lewis Delaney Offeld

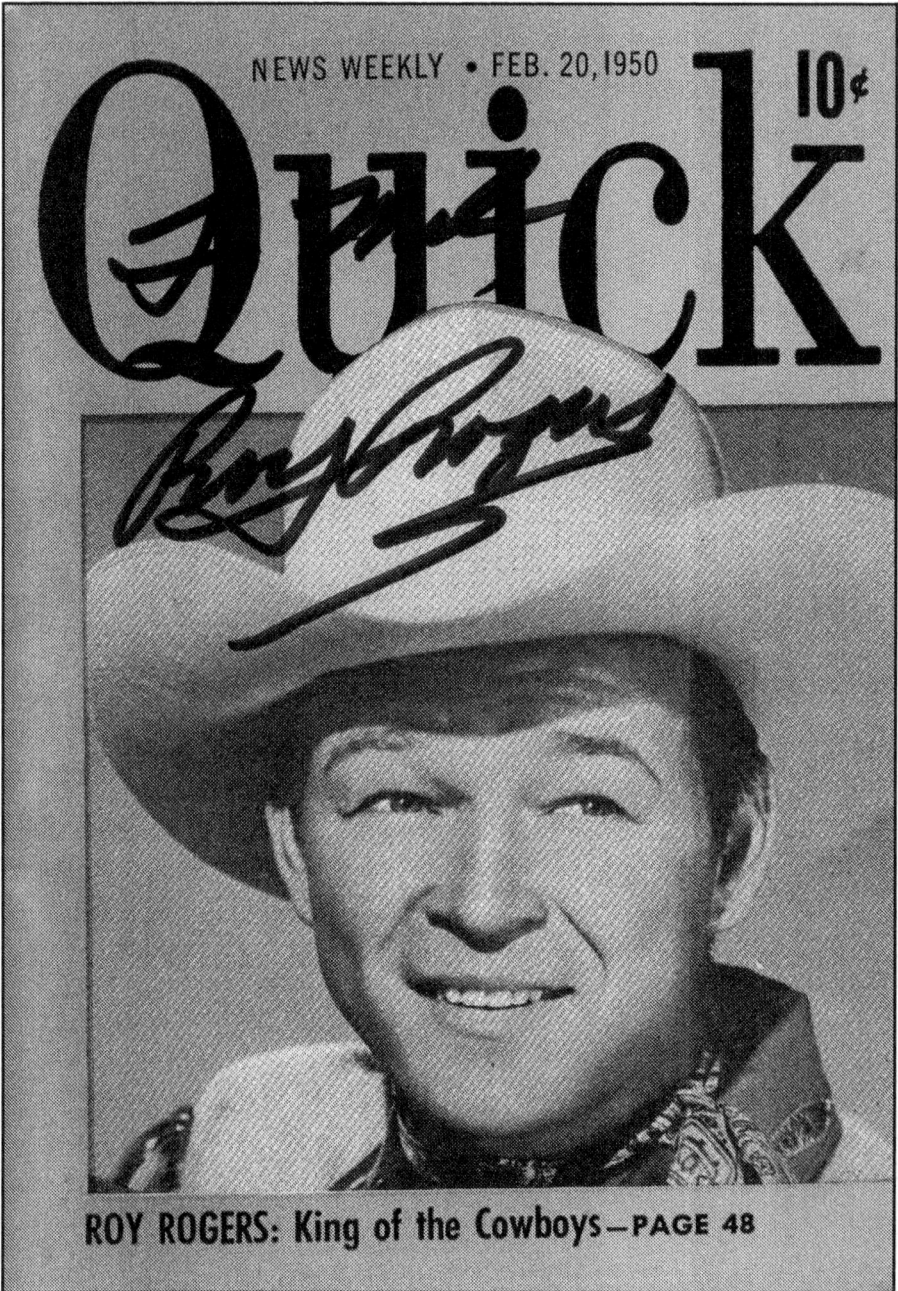

*Roy Rogers*

# Quiz #56

## ROY ROGERS and GENE AUTRY
### Was it Roy or Gene?
*(Answers on page 137)*

1.  Who was born in Cincinnati?
2.  Who was known as Oklahoma's Yodeling Cowboy?
3.  Who sang and played the guitar?
4.  Who recorded for Columbia Records?
5.  Who owned a Major League baseball team, the California Angels?
6.  Whose real name was Leonard Sly?
7.  Who sang with the Sons of the Pioneers?
8.  Who had a dog named Bullet?
9.  Gabby Hayes was a sidekick in the movies for whom?
10. Pat Brady was a sidekick on radio and television for whom?

*Gene Autry*

# Quiz #57

## Match the Tony Award-winning actress with the Broadway musical

*(Answers on page 138)*

1. Chita Rivera
2. Lauren Bacall
3. Diahann Carroll
4. Angela Lansbury
5. Gwen Verdon
6. Patti LuPone
7. Tammy Grimes
8. Dorothy Louden
9. Judy Holliday
10. Barbara Harris

a. *Bells Are Ringing*
b. *The Apple Tree*
c. *Sweeney Todd*
d. *Evita*
e. *No Strings*
f. *Woman of the Year*
g. *The Rink*
h. *The Unsinkable Molly Brown*
i. *Redhead*
j. *Annie*

*Mel Simons &*
*Henny Youngman*

*Mel Simons &*
*Morey Amsterdam*

# Quiz #58

## COMEDIAN QUESTIONS
*(Answers on page 138)*

1. Who was the "King of the One Liners"?
2. Who had a record album, *Child of the Fifties*?
3. Who was married to Edie Adams?
4. Harry Einstein played what character?
5. The song "Rum and Coca-Cola" was written by who?
6. Who starred in *C.P.O Sharkey*?
7. Who was Mike Nichols' original partner?
8. In the movie *The Wizard of Oz*, who played the Cowardly Lion?
9. On George Gobel's television show, what was the name of George's wife?
10. Arthur Lake played what character?

*Steve Allen*

# Quiz #59

## STEVE ALLEN

*(Answers on page 138)*

1.  Steve was born in New York City. Where was he raised?

2.  Steve was the first host of *The Tonight Show*. What years did he host it?

3.  Steve was a regular on what television quiz show?

4.  Steve wrote over 7,000 songs. What was his biggest hit?

5.  Steve hosted what television quiz show from 1964 to 1967?

6.  In the movie of this person's life, Steve played what famous musician?

7.  Steve's second marriage was to what actress?

8.  Steve's mother was a well-known vaudeville comic. What was her name?

9.  Steve's first nationwide television performance was subbing for whom?

10. Steve wrote the lyrics for what famous Dixieland song?

# Quiz #60

## VAUDEVILLE
*(Answers on page 139)*

1.  What did Fred Allen do in vaudeville?

2.  Who was the stuttering comedian?

3.  What were the first names of the Ritz Brothers?

4.  Who was The Street Singer?

5.  What famous television comedian began his career in vaudeville in 1916?

6.  Name the most popular vaudeville theater in England.

7.  Who introduced the song "My Man"?

8.  Name the most famous black comedian in vaudeville.

9.  Who did the routine "Dr. Kronkhite and His Patient"?

10. Who was known as "the man with the rubber legs"?

# Quiz #61

## Match the song with the composer
*(Answers on page 139)*

1. "Always"
2. "Anything Goes"
3. "I Just Called to Say I Love You"
4. "Moon River"
5. "Nine to Five"
6. "Theme from Shaft"
7. "Getting to Know You"
8. "Beautiful Dreamer"
9. "Mama"
10. "Octopus's Garden"

a. Cole Porter
b. Dolly Parton
c. Richard Rodgers and Oscar Hammerstein II
d. Ringo Starr
e. Jerry Herman
f. Irving Berlin
g. Stephen Foster
h. Isaac Hayes
i. Stevie Wonder
j. Johnny Mercer and Henry Mancini

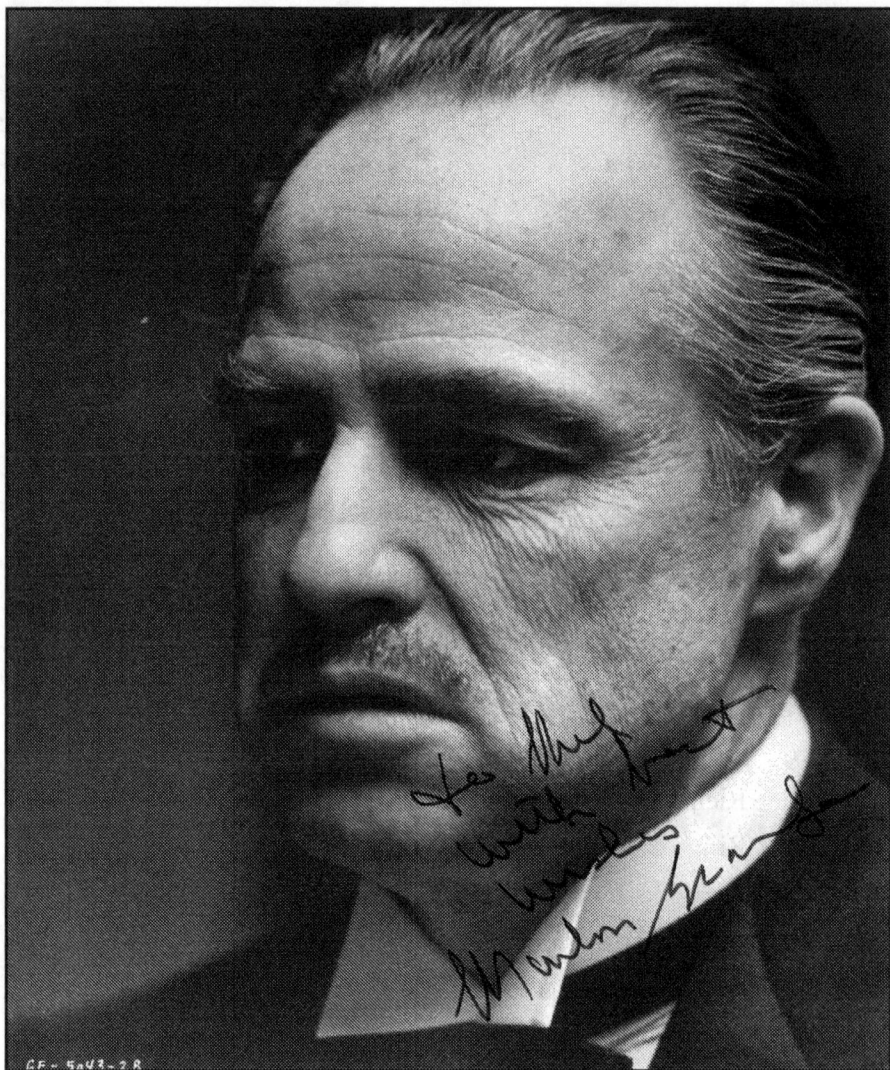

*Marlon Brandon*

# Quiz #62

## MARLON BRANDO
*(Answers on page 140)*

1. What was Brando's first Broadway play?
2. Brando became a star from what Broadway play?
3. What character did he play?
4. Name the movie that won Brando his first Academy Award.
5. Name the movie that won Brando his second Academy Award.
6. Brando sang with Frank Sinatra in what movie?
7. What nickname did Sinatra give Brando?
8. Brando directed one movie. What was it?
9. What was the title of Brando's autobiography?
10. What was the last movie that Brando appeared in?

# Quiz #63

## Match the Academy Award-winning song with the movie

*(Answers on page 140)*

1.  "High Hopes"
2.  "White Christmas"
3.  "Baby, It's Cold Outside"
4.  "Over the Rainbow"
5.  "Talk to the Animals"
6.  "Secret Love"
7.  "Swinging on a Star"
8.  "Thanks for the Memory"
9.  "All the Way"
10. "Mona Lisa"


a.  *The Wizard of Oz*
b.  *Calamity Jane*
c.  *The Joker Is Wild*
d.  *Holiday Inn*
e.  *A Hole in the Head*
f.  *Neptune's Daughter*
g.  *Doctor Doolittle*
h.  *Captain Carey, U.S.A.*
i.  *Going My Way*
j.  *Big Broadcast of 1938*

# Quiz #64

## SILENT MOVIES
*(Answers on page 140)*

1. Who was the first Tarzan?
2. Who was Douglas Fairbanks married to?
3. What comedian was cross eyed?
4. Who starred in *Dr. Jekyll and Mr. Hyde*?
5. What comedian hung from a clock?
6. Who produced *The Ten Commandments*?
7. What comedian was known as a lovable, confused little man?
8. Name the two most popular cowboys.
9. Who was the most successful silent movie director?
10. Name Rudolph Valentino's last movie.

Guy Lombardo

# Quiz #65

## Match the bandleader with his vocalist

*(Answers on page 141)*

1. Glenn Miller
2. Benny Goodman
3. Tommy Dorsey
4. Guy Lombardo
5. Harry James
6. Sammy Kaye
7. Lawrence Welk
8. Les Brown
9. Ted Weems
10. Jimmy Dorsey

a. Doris Day
b. Perry Como
c. Don Cornell
d. Ray Eberle
e. Jo Stafford
f. Bob Eberly
g. Helen Forrest
h. Peggy Lee
i. Kenny Gardner
j. Norma Zimmer

*Sammy Kaye*

*Don Cornell*

*The Andrews Sisters*

# Quiz #66

## Name the sister vocal groups with their hit record
*(Answers on page 141)*

1.  "Beer Barrel Polka"
2.  "Sincerely"
3.  "Teach Me Tonight"
4.  "Seventeen"
5.  "Rum and Coca-Cola"
6.  "Tonight You Belong to Me"
7.  "Hearts of Stone"
8.  "May You Always"
9.  "No More"
10. "Bei Mir Bist Du Schoen"

*The McGuire Sisters*

# Quiz #67

## COMEDIAN QUESTIONS

*(Answers on page 142)*

1. Who founded St. Jude's Hospital?

2. The character, Ernestine, was played by whom?

3. What comedian starred in *Bye Bye Birdie*?

4. Who was George Burns' closest friend?

5. Who is Joseph A. Gottlieb?

6. Who was the leader of the Bowery Boys?

7. Foster Brooks is best known for playing what type of character?

8. What lady always tugged her ear at the end of her television show?

9. Howard Morris was a second banana to whom?

10. What comedian appeared the most on *The Ed Sullivan Show*?

*Perry Como*

# Quiz #68

## PERRY COMO

*(Answers on page 142)*

1. Before he became a singer, what did Perry do for a living?
2. What big band did Perry sing with?
3. What was Perry's first hit record?
4. What was Perry's first number one record?
5. Perry recorded with what female vocal group?
6. Name Perry's biggest selling Christmas song.
7. Who sponsored Perry's radio show?
8. What night of the week was his television show on?
9. What was Perry's last top ten record?
10. Name Perry's theme song.

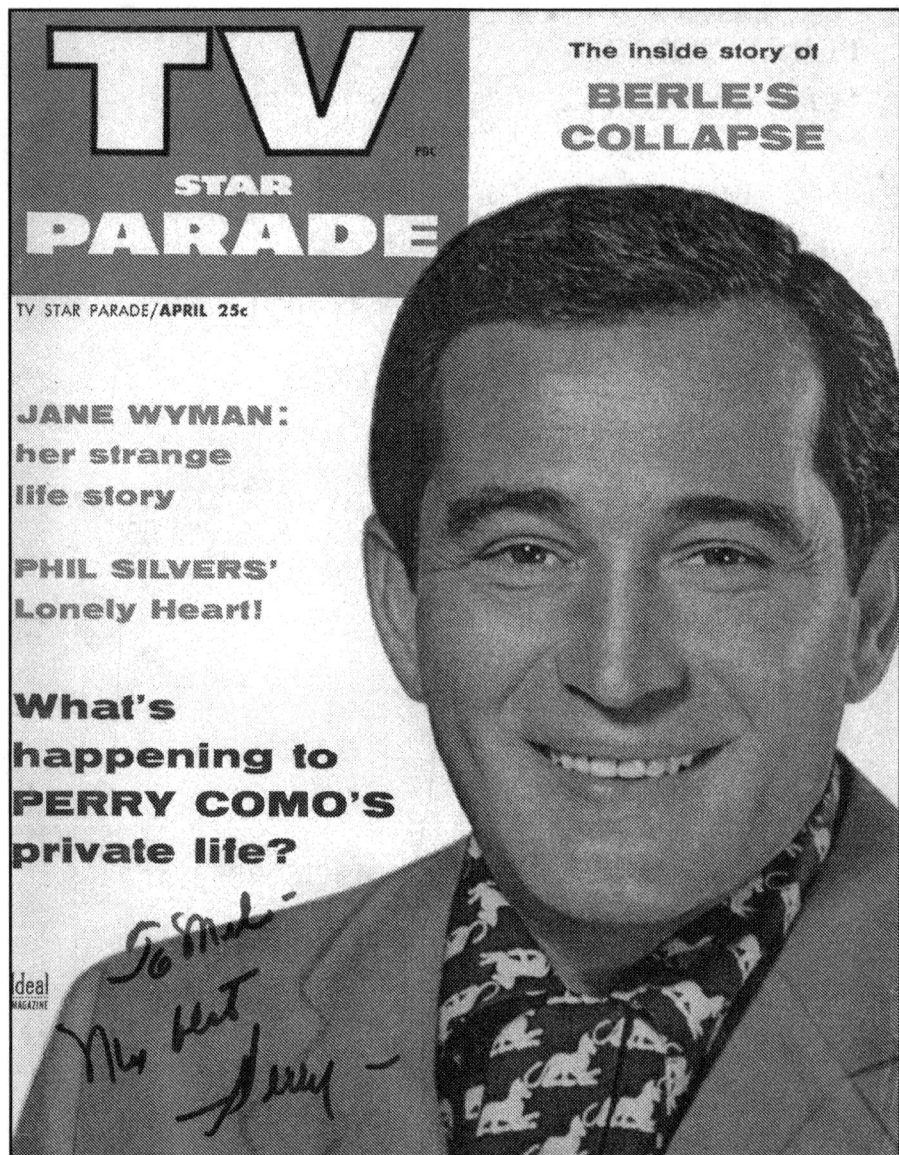

TV STAR PARADE

The inside story of **BERLE'S COLLAPSE**

STAR PARADE

TV STAR PARADE/**APRIL 25¢**

**JANE WYMAN:** her strange life story

**PHIL SILVERS'** Lonely Heart!

**What's happening to PERRY COMO'S private life?**

ideal MAGAZINE

# Quiz #69

## Match the Academy Award-winning director with the movie

*(Answers on page 142)*

1. Billy Wilder
2. William Wyler
3. George Cukor
4. John Schlesinger
5. Michael Curtiz
6. Fred Zimmerman
7. William Friedkin
8. Bob Fosse
9. Vincent Minnelli
10. Mike Nichols


a. *My Fair Lady*
b. *The French Connection*
c. *From Here to Eternity*
d. *Gigi*
e. *Midnight Cowboy*
f. *The Apartment*
g. *Ben-Hur*
h. *Casablanca*
i. *The Graduate*
j. *Cabaret*

*George Burns*

# Quiz #70

## GEORGE BURNS
*(Answers on page 143)*

1. What is George's birth name?
2. How many brothers and sisters did he have?
3. What was the name of the vocal group that George sang with as a kid?
4. What was the first movie that Burns and Allen appeared in?
5. Burns and Allen began their radio career with what bandleader?
6. On the Burns and Allen radio show, who was the announcer?
7. On the Burns and Allen radio show, who was the Happy Postman?
8. On the Burns and Allen television show, name the two Harrys.
9. George won the Academy Award as Best Supporting Actor in what movie?
10. How old was he when he won the Academy Award?

# ANSWERS

## Quiz #1  *(from page 1)*

1. Paris, France
2. 12 years old
3. He was an acrobat
4. A straw hat
5. "Louise"
6. "Louise"
7. *Monkey Business*
8. Jeanette MacDonald
9. *With Love*
10. "I Remember It Well"

## Quiz #2  *(from page 2)*

1. d
2. j
3. e
4. f
5. h
6. I
7. a
8. c
9. g
10. b

## Quiz #3  *(from page 3)*

1. d
2. e
3. g
4. a
5. f
6. j
7. I
8. h
9. c
10. b

## Quiz #4  *(from page 5)*

1. Pennsylvania
2. MGM
3. *The Philadelphia Story*
4. Air Force
5. George Bailey
6. Glenn Miller
7. *The Greatest Show on Earth*
8. Five times
9. *The Six Shooter*
10. *The Man Who Knew Too Much*

## Quiz #5  *(from page 6)*

1. Debbie Reynolds and The Ames Brothers
2. Dick Contino
3. Les Paul and Mary Ford
4. Georgia Gibbs
5. Martha Tilton

6. The DeJohn Sisters
7. Aretha Franklin
8. B.B. King
9. James Brown
10. The Chordettes

# Quiz #6 *(from page 7)*
1. e
2. c
3. g
4. h
5. d
6. I
7. a
8. b
9. f
10. j

# Quiz #7 *(from page 9)*
1. Herbert John Gleason
2. He did stand-up comedy in nightclubs
3. *Springtime in the Rockies* and *Orchestra Wives*
4. *The Life of Riley*
5. *Cavalcade of Stars*
6. Ed Norton
7. Crazy Guggenheim
8. *The Hustler*
9. Jane Kean
10. "And awaaaaaaay we go!"

## Quiz #8 *(from page 11)*

1. Trumpet
2. Saxophone
3. Piano
4. Drums
5. Trombone
6. Piano
7. Trumpet
8. Saxophone
9. Drums
10. Trumpet

## Quiz #9 *(from page 12)*

1. f
2. b
3. I
4. a
5. j
6. g
7. c
8. h
9. d
10. e

## Quiz #10 *(from page 13)*

1. Mel Blanc
2. Tubby
3. Olive Oil
4. Jerry the Mouse
5. Mickey Mouse's original name.

6. Hamburgers
7. Mr. Magoo
8. Steamboat Willie (1932)
9. Tweety
10. Arthur Q. Bryan

## Quiz #11 *(from page 15)*

1. Marion Michael Morrison
2. Los Angeles, California
3. "Duke"
4. Football
5. University of Southern California
6. Tom Mix
7. *Stagecoach*
8. *Rio Grande, The Quiet Man, The Wings of Eagles, McLintock!, Big Jake.*
9. *True Grit*
10. Warner Brothers

## Quiz #12 *(from page 16)*

1. g
2. a
3. I
4. h
5. c
6. d
7. b
8. j
9. f
10. e

## Quiz #13 *(from page 17)*

1. I
2. c
3. b
4. a
5. f
6. g
7. d
8. e
9. h
10. j

## Quiz #14 *(from page 19)*

1. g
2. e
3. d
4. h
5. c
6. j
7. b
8. I
9. a
10. f

## Quiz #15 *(from page 21)*

1. New York City
2. Boston
3. Chicago
4. Philadelphia
5. Pittsburg

6. Buffalo
7. Las Vegas
8. Brooklyn
9. Chicago
10. Windsor, Ontario

## Quiz #16 *(from page 23)*
1. Albert
2. The Hoboken Four
3. *Major Bowes and His Original Amateur Hour*
4. Four times
5. Three children
6. Harry James and Tommy Dorsey
7. "I'll Never Smile Again"
8. *Your Hit Parade*
9. Maggio
10. "Somethin' Stupid" (with his daughter, Nancy)

## Quiz #17 *(from page 25)*
1. c
2. j
3. e
4. d
5. b
6. I
7. h
8. f
9. a
10. g

## Quiz #18  *(from page 27)*
1. George Steele
2. Killer Kowalski
3. Ric Flair and Buddy Rogers
4. Argentina
5. Chief Jay Strongbow
6. Gorgeous George
7. Andre the Giant
8. Bruno Sammartino
9. Lou Thesz
10. The Bear Hug

## Quiz #19  *(from page 29)*
1. Tacoma, Washington
2. Harry Lillis Crosby
3. Paul Whiteman
4. The Rhythm Boys
5. Dixie Lee and Kathryn
6. Seven (four by his first wife, and three by his second wife)
7. *Going My Way*
8. A priest
9. *The Hollywood Palace*
10. "White Christmas"

## Quiz #20  *(from page 30)*
1. e
2. d
3. f
4. b
5. I

6. j
7. h
8. c
9. a
10. g

# Quiz #21 *(from page 31)*
1. Jack Armstrong
2. *Little Orphan Annie*
3. Mel Blanc
4. The Sportsman Quartet
5. Lawrence Tibbett
6. Doc Gamble
7. The DeMarco Sisters
8. The Organ
9. The Falcon
10. Oogie Pringle

# Quiz #22 *(from page 33)*
1. c
2. b
3. g
4. e
5. a
6. d
7. j
8. I
9. f
10. h

## Quiz #23  *(from page 35)*

1. e
2. g
3. h
4. b
5. I
6. c
7. f
8. j
9. a
10. d

## Quiz #24  *(from page 37)*

1. The Little Tramp
2. Mack Sennett
3. *Making a Living*
4. Mary Pickford, Douglas Fairbanks, and D.W. Griffith
5. *The Gold Rush* (1925)
6. *Modern Times*
7. *The Great Dictator* (1940)
8. *Limelight* (1952)
9. "Smile"
10. Robert Downey, Jr.

## Quiz #25  *(from page 39)*

1. Both
2. Both
3. Sedaka
4. Sedaka
5. Sedaka

6. Diamond
7. Diamond
8. Sedaka
9. Sedaka
10. A tie. Both had three #1 records:
Neil Diamond:
1970 – "Cracklin' Rosie"
1972 – "Song Sung Blue"
1978 – "You Don't Bring Me Flowers" (with Barbra Streisand)

Neil Sedaka:
1962 – "Breaking Up Is Hard To Do"
1974 – "Laughter in the Rain"
1975 – "Bad Blood"

# Quiz #26 *(from page 41)*
1. David
2. Jay
3. David
4. David
5. Jay
6. David
7. David (one son)
8. David
9. Jay
10. Jay

## Quiz #27  *(from page 43)*
1. Dancing
2. Barney Rapp, Bob Crosby and Les Brown
3. "Sentimental Journey" and "My Dreams Are Getting Better All the Time"
4. *The Man Who Knew Too Much*
5. *Young at Heart*
6. "Secret Love"
7. "Whatever Will Be Will Be (Que Sera, Sera)"
8. Doris Martin
9. Ruth Etting
10. "Everybody Loves a Lover"

## Quiz #28  *(from page 45)*
1. d
2. a
3. b
4. h
5. j
6. I
7. e
8. f
9. g
10. c

## Quiz #29  *(from page 46)*
1. Fanny Brice
2. The Maxwell
3. Rexall
4. Mike Clancy
5. Cecil B. DeMille

6. Irma Peterson
7. Bob Swan
8. Jane
9. *Big Town*
10. J. Scott Smart

## Quiz #30  *(from page 47)*
1. The Palace Theater in New York
2. *The Ziegfeld Follies*
3. Sophie Tucker
4. He was a juggler
5. Ted Lewis
6. Eddie Cantor
7. Frank Fay
8. Minnie
9. Will Rogers
10. George Jessel

## Quiz #31  *(from page 49)*
1. Gene
2. Gene
3. Fred
4. Fred
5. Fred
6. Fred
7. Both
8. Gene
9. Gene
10. Fred

## Quiz #32 *(from page 51)*

1. e
2. d
3. g
4. h
5. b
6. f
7. a
8. I
9. c
10. j

## Quiz #33 *(from page 53)*

1. Mary Tyler Moore
2. Phyllis Diller
3. Totie Fields
4. Mae West
5. Joan Rivers
6. Lily Tomlin
7. Molly Goldberg
8. Moms Mabley
9. Gracie Allen
10. Baby Snooks

## Quiz #34 *(from page 55)*

1. Ted Healy
2. Harry Moses, Jerome and Samuel Horwitz
3. Louis Feinberg
4. Violin
5. 196

6.  1932 – 1947
7.  Curly
8.  Joe Besser
9.  Curly Joe DeRita – Joseph Wardell
10. "Three Blind Mice"

# Quiz #35  *(from page 57)*
1.  Two times
2.  *Suspicion, Notorious, To Catch a Thief, North by Northwest*
3.  *North by Northwest*
4.  *That Touch of Mink*
5.  Frank Sinatra
6.  *To Catch a Thief*
7.  Five times
8.  Barbara Hutton
9.  Dyan Cannon
10. One (daughter Jennifer)

# Quiz #36  *(from page 58)*
1.  Jock Mahoney
2.  William Boyd
3.  Gene Autry
4.  *Gunsmoke* (20 years)
5.  *Bonanza* (16 years)
6.  Gene Autry
7.  Lash LaRue
8.  California
9.  Andy Clyde
10. Cartwright

## Quiz #37  *(from page 59)*

1. a
2. c
3. g
4. h
5. f
6. i
7. j
8. b
9. d
10. e

## Quiz #38  *(from page 61)*

1. Schnozzola
2. "Inka Dinka Doo"
3. Clayton, Jackson, and Durante
4. The Club Durant
5. Garry Moore
6. *Jumbo*
7. *Bill Rose's Jumbo*
8. "September Song"
9. *It's a Mad, Mad, Mad, Mad World*
10. Mrs. Callabash

## Quiz #39  *(from page 63)*

1. The Four Aces
2. The Four Lads
3. The Ames Brothers
4. The Four Aces
5. The Four Preps

6.  The Ames Brothers
7.  The Four Lads
8.  The Four Preps
9.  The Four Coins
10. The Four Aces

## Quiz #40 *(from page 64)*
1.  *Our Miss Brooks*
2.  School teacher
3.  Bert Gordon
4.  Sylvia
5.  Joe E. Lewis
6.  Bill Cosby
7.  Merwyn Bogue
8.  Joe E. Brown
9.  Sam Levenson
10. Brad

## Quiz #41 *(from page 65)*
1.  j
2.  i
3.  h
4.  g
5.  f
6.  e
7.  d
8.  c
9.  b
10. a

## Quiz #42  *(from page 67)*
1. 1927
2. Charlie Chaplin
3. Norvell
4. Babe
5. Hardy
6. *The Music Box* (1932)
7. "Waltz of the Cuckoos"
8. Stan
9. Hal Roach
10. "Sons of the Desert"

## Quiz #43  *(from page 69)*
1. b
2. f
3. d
4. c
5. a
6. e
7. j
8. i
9. h
10. g

## Quiz #44  *(from page 71)*
1. Israel Iskowitz
2. Ida
3. "Banjo Eyes"
4. Florenz Ziegfeld
5. 1917

6.  Rudy Vallee's *Fleischmann's Yeast Hour*
7.  The March of Dimes
8.  Dinah Shore
9.  *Colgate Comedy Hour*
10. Keefe Brasselle


# Quiz #45  *(from page 72)*
1.  i
2.  h
3.  f
4.  c
5.  d
6.  b
7.  e
8.  g
9.  a
10. j


# Quiz #46  *(from page 73)*
1.  g
2.  i
3.  j
4.  a
5.  d
6.  h
7.  c
8.  e
9.  b
10. f

## Quiz #47  *(from page 75)*
1. Ethel
2. Ethel
3. Mary
4. Mary
5. Ethel
6. Mary
7. Mary
8. Ethel
9. Ethel
10. Ethel

## Quiz #48  *(from page 77)*
1. He owned an antique shop.
2. Birdie
3. Homer Brown
4. Insurance Investigator
5. Jack Webb
6. Bob Burns
7. Lipton Tea and Lipton Soup
8. *Suspense*
9. Minerva Pious
10. Johnny

## Quiz #49  *(from page 79)*
1. e
2. j
3. c
4. i
5. a

6. h
7. g
8. f
9. d
10. b

# Quiz #50 *(from page 81)*
1. 1925
2. His father
3. Will Mastin Trio
4. *Mr. Wonderful*
5. The Rat Pack
6. Judaism
7. *Yes I Can*
8. May Britt & Altovise Gore
9. *Golden Boy*
10. "The Candy Man" (1972)

# Quiz #51 *(from page 82)*
1. a
2. d
3. e
4. b
5. f
6. j
7. i
8. c
9. g
10. h

## Quiz #52   *(from page 83)*

1.  c
2.  f
3.  a
4.  h
5.  j
6.  b
7.  g
8.  i
9.  d
10. e

## Quiz #53   *(from page 85)*

1.  New York City
2.  Vaudeville and Broadway
3.  5'5" tall
4.  *The Public Enemy*
5.  He pushed a grapefruit in her face
6.  *Yankee Doodle Dandy*
7.  George M. Cohan
8.  He never said it
9.  Jeanne Cagney
10. *Love Me or Leave Me*

## Quiz #54   *(from page 86)*

1.  Charlie Chaplin
2.  Laurel and Hardy
3.  Clara Bow
4.  Lon Chaney
5.  *The Great Train Robbery*

6. Mary Pickford
7. Dorothy
8. Edgar Kennedy
9. Pearl White
10. Buster Keaton

# Quiz #55 *(from page 87)*
1. d
2. g
3. h
4. j
5. b
6. i
7. a
8. e
9. c
10. f

# Quiz #56 *(from page 89)*
1. Roy
2. Gene
3. Both
4. Gene
5. Gene
6. Roy
7. Roy
8. Roy
9. Roy
10. Roy

## Quiz #57  *(from page 91)*

1. g
2. f
3. e
4. c
5. i
6. d
7. h
8. j
9. a
10. b

## Quiz #58  *(from page 93)*

1. Henny Youngman
2. Robert Klein
3. Ernie Kovacs
4. Parkyakarkus
5. Morey Amsterdam
6. Don Rickles
7. Elaine May
8. Bert Lahr
9. Alice
10. Dagwood Bumstead

## Quiz #59  *(from page 95)*

1. Chicago
2. 1954-1957
3. *What's My Line?*
4. "This Could Be the Start of Something Big"
5. *What's My Line?*

6. Benny Goodman
7. Jayne Meadows
8. Belle Montrose
9. Arthur Godfrey
10. "South Rampart Street Parade"

## Quiz #60  *(from page 96)*

1. He was a comedy juggler
2. Joe Frisco
3. Harry, Al, Jimmy
4. Arthur Tracy
5. Milton Berle
6. The London Palladium
7. Fannie Brice
8. Bert Williams
9. Smith and Dale
10. Leon Errol

## Quiz #61  *(from page 97)*

1. f
2. a
3. i
4. j
5. b
6. h
7. c
8. g
9. e
10. d

## Quiz #62  *(from page 99)*
1. *I Remember Mama*
2. *A Streetcar Named Desire*
3. Stanley Kowalski
4. *On the Waterfront* (1954)
5. *The Godfather* (1972)
6. *Guys and Dolls*
7. Mumbles
8. *One-Eyed Jacks*
9. *Songs My Mother Taught Me*
10. *The Score* (2001)

## Quiz #63  *(from page 100)*
1. e
2. d
3. f
4. a
5. g
6. b
7. i
8. j
9. c
10. h

## Quiz #64  *(from page 101)*
1. Elmo Lincoln
2. Mary Pickford
3. Ben Turpin
4. John Barrymore
5. Harold Lloyd

6. Cecil B. DeMille
7. Harry Langdon
8. Tom Mix and William H. Hart
9. D.W. Griffith
10. *Son of the Sheik*

## Quiz #65 *(from page 103)*

1. d
2. h
3. e
4. i
5. g
6. c
7. j
8. a
9. b
10. f

## Quiz #66 *(from page 105)*

1. Andrews Sisters
2. McGuire Sisters
3. DeCastro Sisters
4. Fontaine Sisters
5. Andrews Sisters
6. Lennon Sisters
7. Fontaine Sisters
8. McGuire Sisters
9. DeJohn Sisters
10. Andrews Sisters

## Quiz #67  *(from page 107)*
1. Danny Thomas
2. Lily Tomlin
3. Dick Van Dyke
4. Jack Benny
5. Joey Bishop
6. Leo Gorcey
7. A drunk
8. Carol Burnett
9. Sid Caesar
10. Alan King

## Quiz #68  *(from page 109)*
1. He was a barber
2. Ted Weems
3. "Long Ago and Far Away"
4. "Till the End of Time"
5. The Fontaine Sisters
6. "Home for the Holidays"
7. Chesterfield
8. Saturday
9. "It's Impossible"
10. "Dream Along With Me"

## Quiz #69  *(from page 111)*
1. f
2. g
3. a
4. e
5. h

6. c
7. b
8. j
9. d
10. i


# Quiz #70 *(from page 113)*

1. Nathan Birnbaum
2. Eleven
3. The Pee Wee Quartet
4. *The Big Broadcast* (1932)
5. Guy Lombardo
6. Bill Goodwin
7. Mel Blanc
8. Harry Morton and Harry Von Zell
9. *The Sunshine Boys*
10. Eighty years old